# POPUL PROBLEMS

# LEONARD

**Staffordshire Library and Information Services**
Please return or renew by the last date shown

24 Hour Renewal Line
0845 33 00 740

If not required by other readers, this item may be renewed in person, by post or telephone, online or by email. To renew, either the book or ticket are required.

Staffordshire County Council

BIDDULPH
Tunstall Road, Biddulph
Staffordshire ST8 6HH
Tel: 01782 485491

14 DEC
5 JAN 2
26 JAN
16 173
06/18

NEWCASTLE

Published by
Wise Publications
14-15 Berners Street, London W1T 3LJ, UK.

Exclusive Distributors:
Music Sales Limited
Distribution Centre, Newmarket Road,
Bury St Edmunds, Suffolk IP33 3YB, UK.
Music Sales Corporation
180 Madison Avenue, 24th Floor,
New York NY 10016, USA.
Music Sales Pty Limited
Units 3-4, 17 Willfox Street, Condell Park,
NSW 2200, Australia.

Order No. AM1010174
ISBN: 978-1-78305-862-4
This book © Copyright 2014 Wise Publications,
a division of Music Sales Limited.

Unauthorised reproduction of any part of this publication by
any means including photocopying is an infringement of copyright.

Edited by Jenni Norey.
Music arranged by Alistair Watson.
Music processed by Paul Ewers Music Design.

Printed in the EU.

SLOW 6
ALMOST LIKE THE BLUES 12
SAMSON IN NEW ORLEANS 36
A STREET 16
DID I EVER LOVE YOU 20
MY OH MY 26
NEVERMIND 30
BORN IN CHAINS 41
YOU GOT ME SINGING 48

# SLOW

Words & Music by Leonard Cohen & Patrick Leonard

# ALMOST LIKE THE BLUES

Words & Music by Leonard Cohen & Patrick Leonard

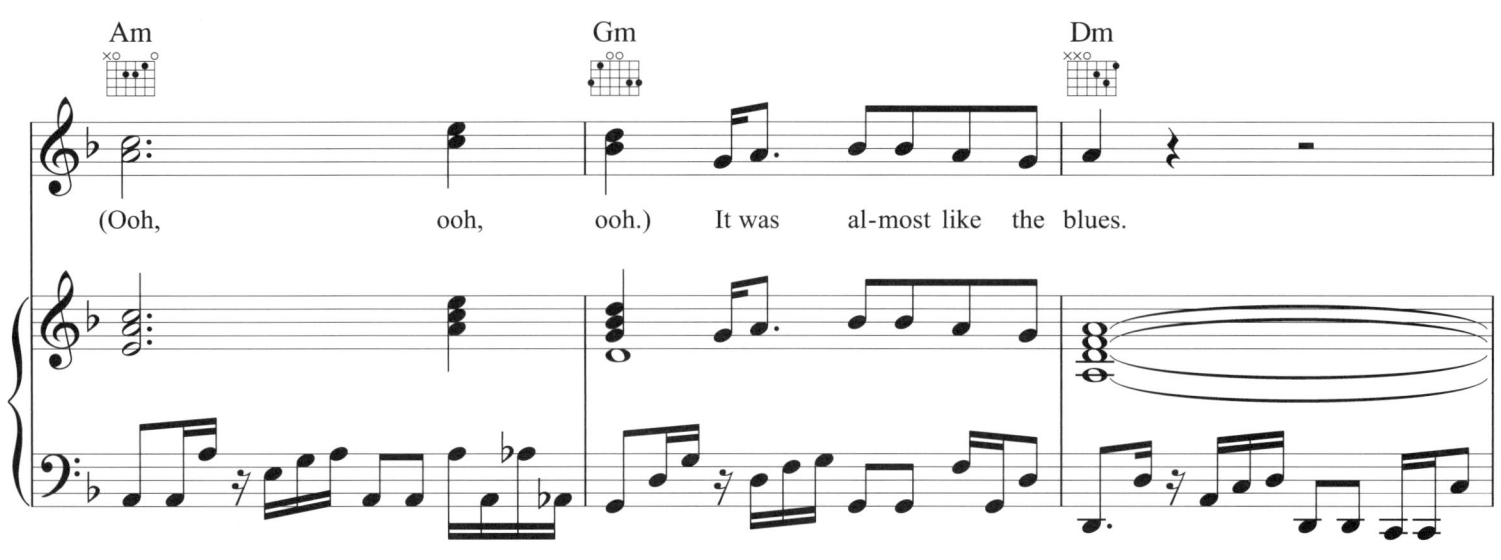

# A STREET

Words & Music by Leonard Cohen & Anjani Thomas

# DID I EVER LOVE YOU

Words & Music by Leonard Cohen & Patrick Leonard

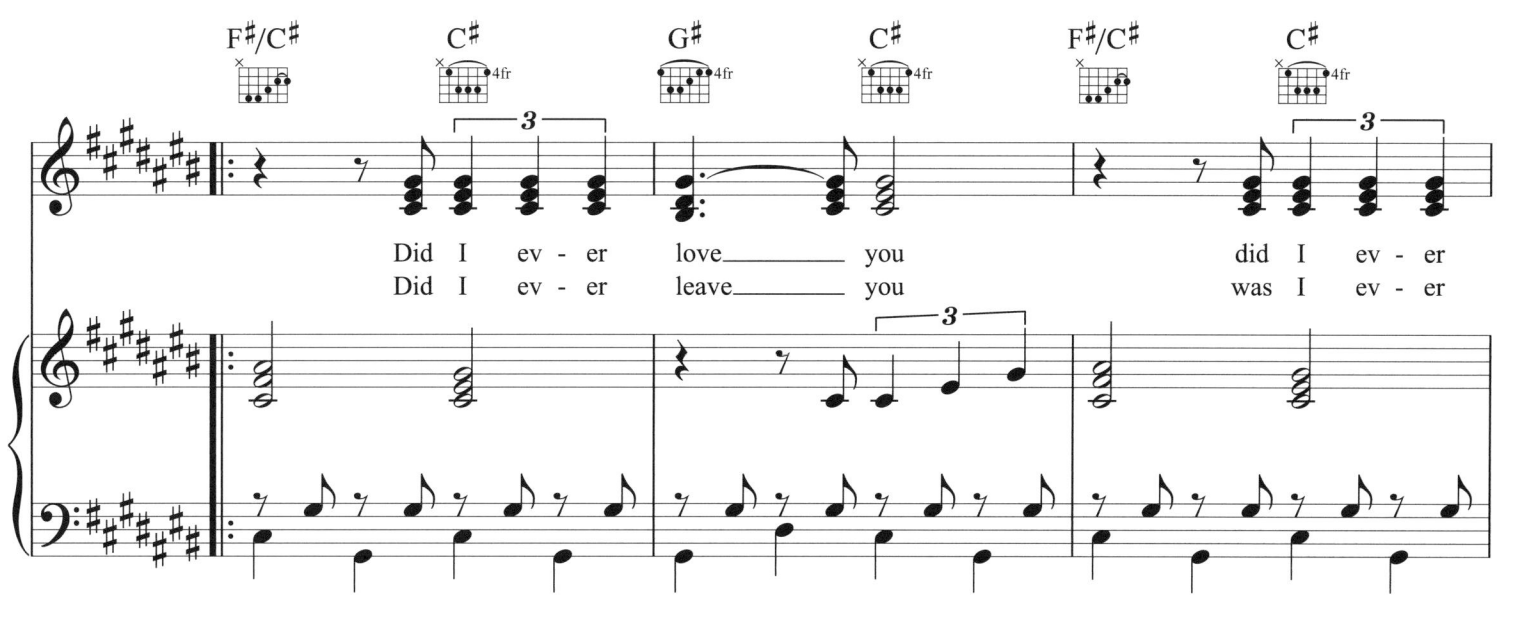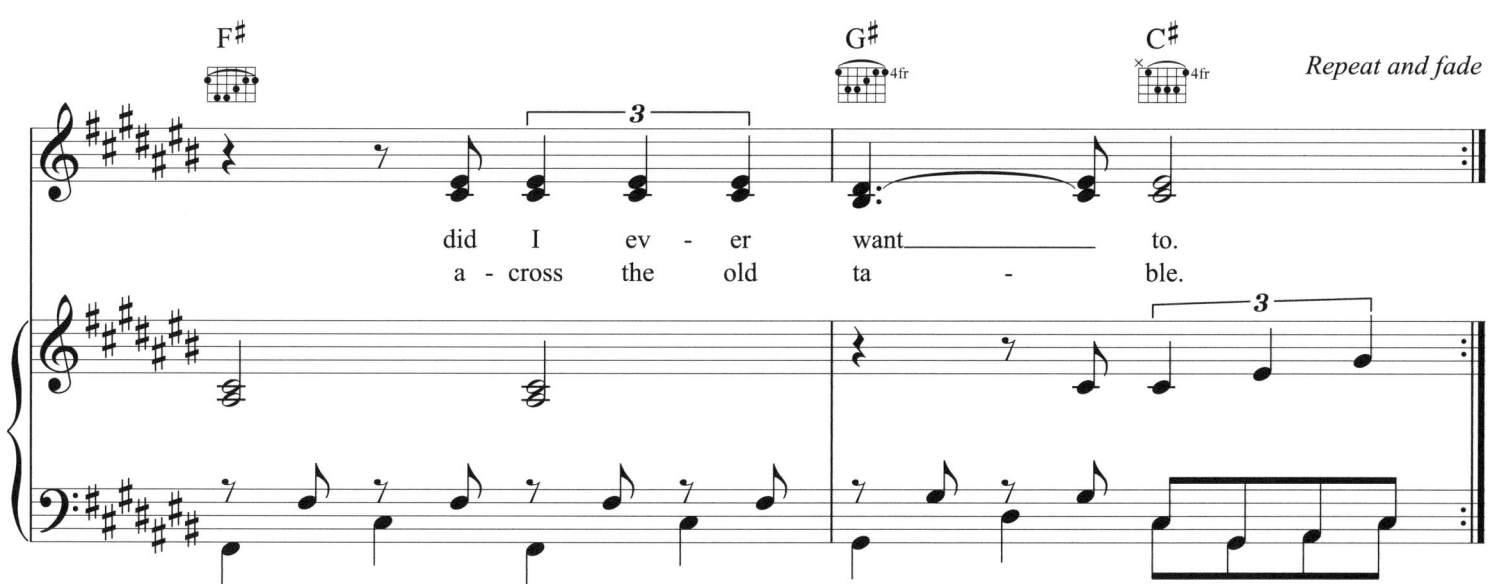

# MY OH MY

Words & Music by Leonard Cohen & Patrick Leonard

# NEVERMIND

Words & Music by Leonard Cohen & Patrick Leonard

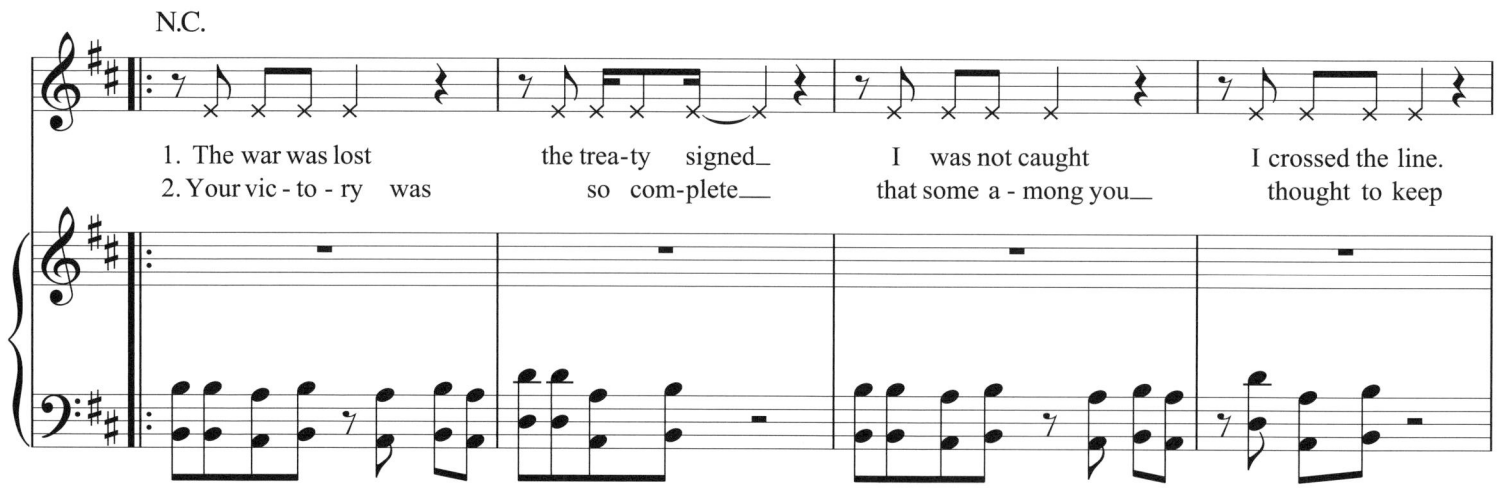

1. The war was lost the trea-ty signed I was not caught I crossed the line.
2. Your vic-to-ry was so com-plete that some a-mong you thought to keep

I was not caught though man-y tried I live a-mong you well dis-guised.
a re-cord of our lit-tle lives. The clothes we wore our spoons our knives.

© Copyright 2014 No Tomato Music/Old Ideas, LLC.
Sony/ATV Music Publishing/Kobalt Music Publishing Limited.
All Rights Reserved. International Copyright Secured.

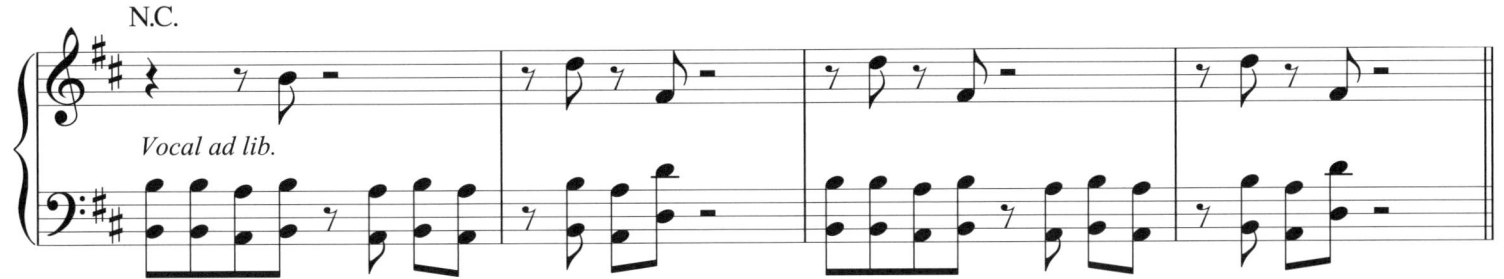

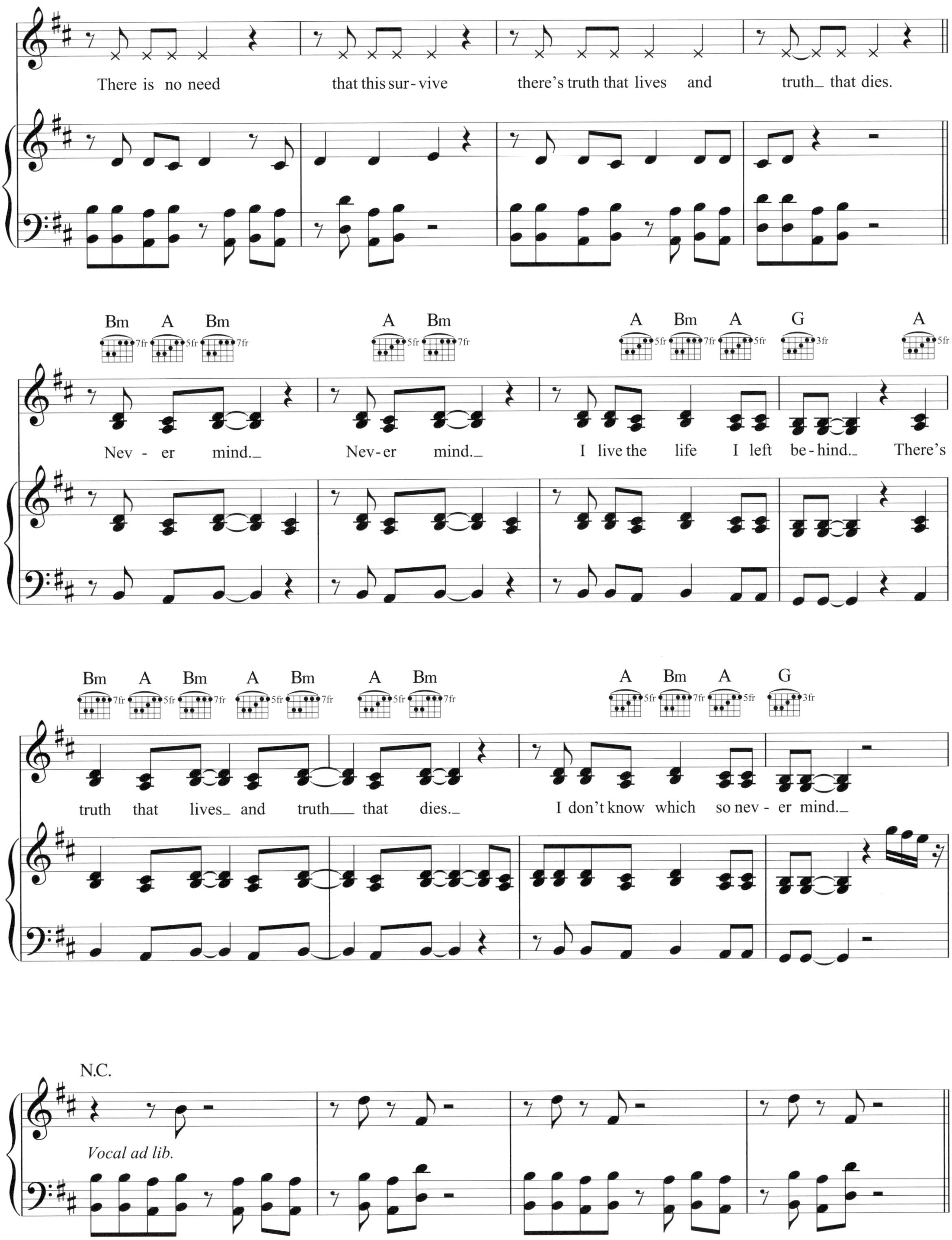
There is no need that this sur-vive there's truth that lives and truth_ that dies.
Bm A Bm A Bm A Bm A G A
Nev - er mind._ Nev-er mind._ I live the life I left be-hind._ There's
Bm A Bm A Bm A Bm A Bm A G
truth that lives_ and truth__ that dies._ I don't know which so nev - er mind._
N.C.
Vocal ad lib.

# SAMSON IN NEW ORLEANS

Words & Music by Leonard Cohen & Patrick Leonard

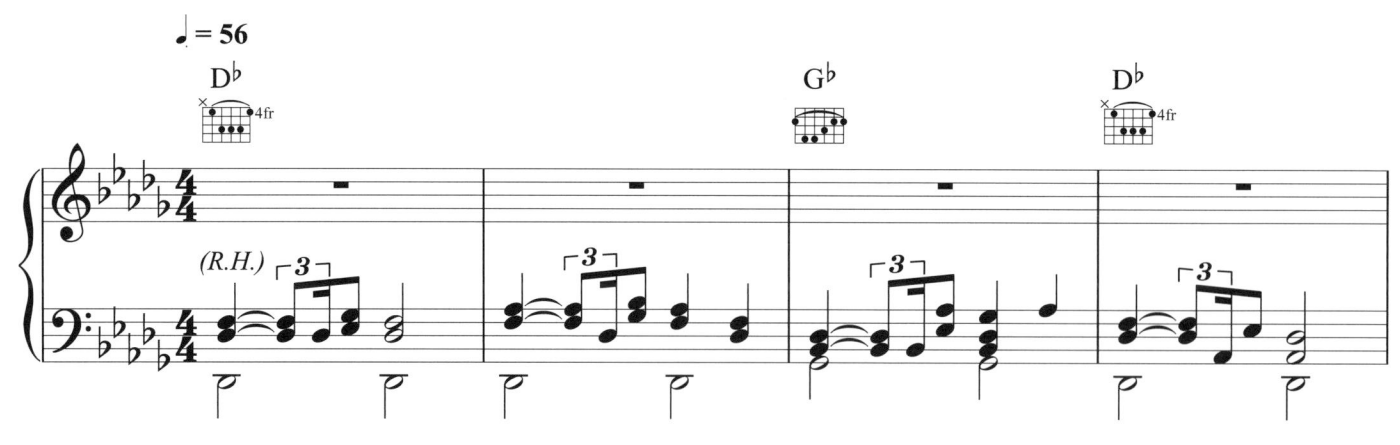

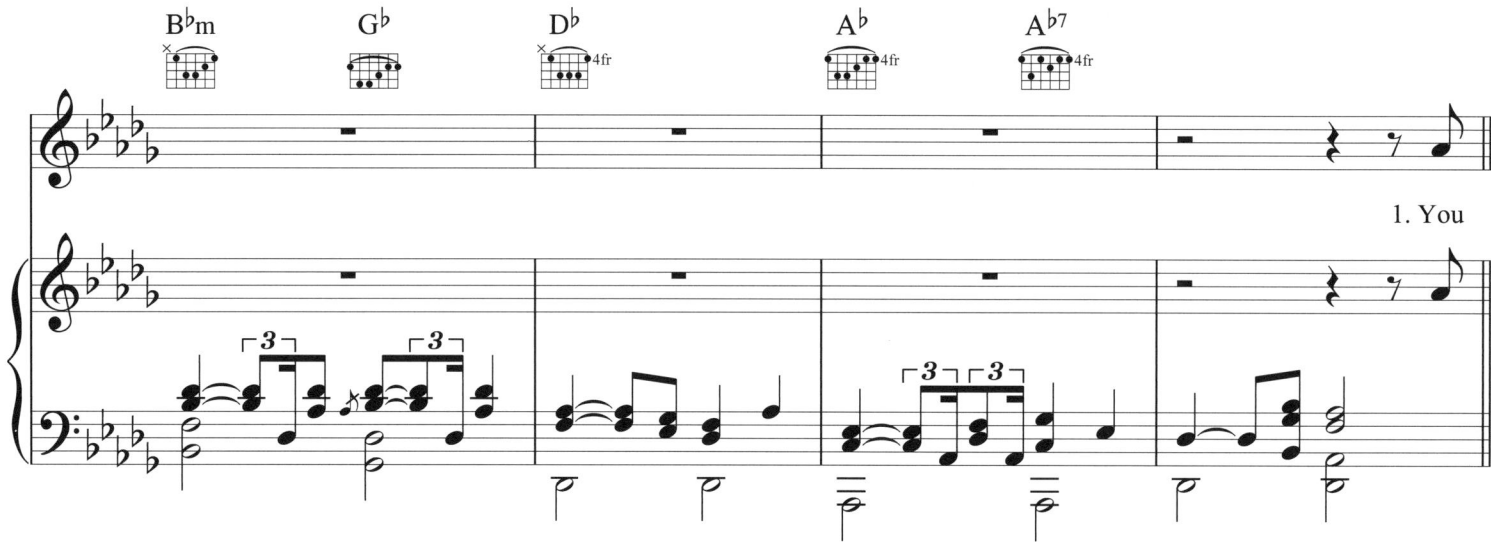

said that you___ were with me   you said you were my friend,   did you
(2.) said how___ could this hap-pen   you said how___ can this be,___   the

© Copyright 2014 No Tomato Music/Old Ideas, LLC.
Sony/ATV Music Publishing/Kobalt Music Publishing Limited.
All Rights Reserved. International Copyright Secured.

# YOU GOT ME SINGING

Words & Music by Leonard Cohen & Patrick Leonard

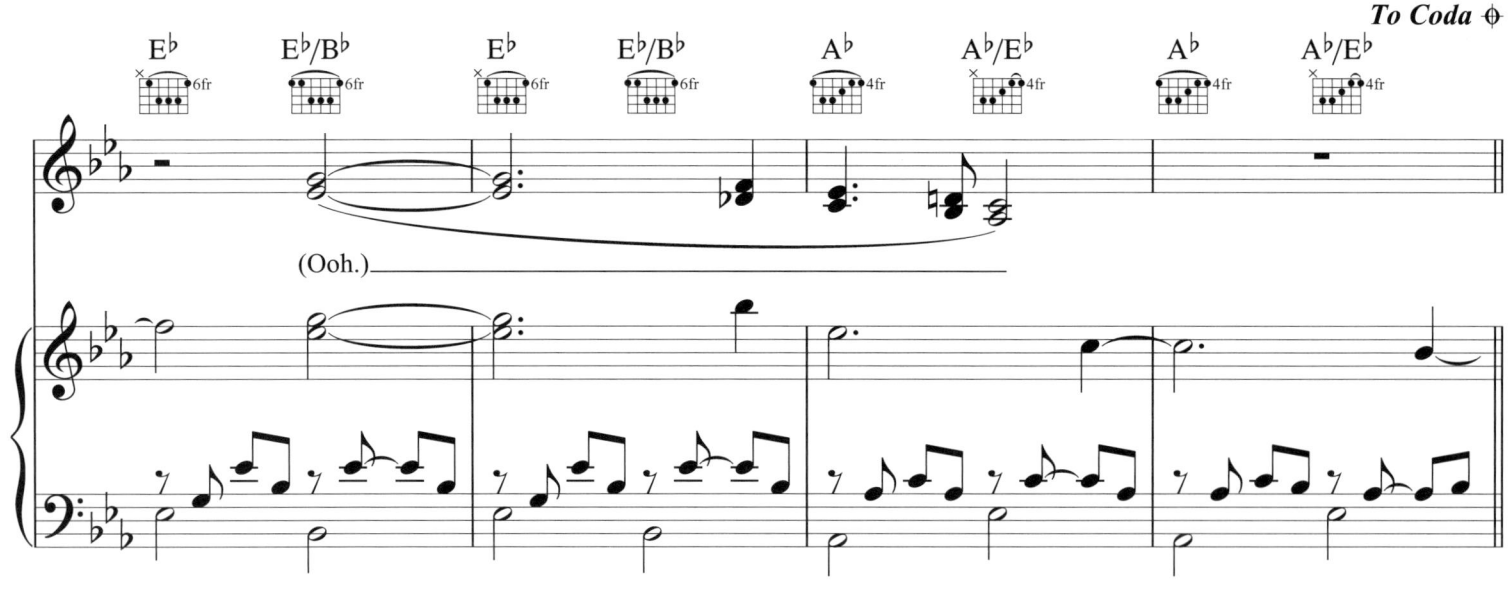
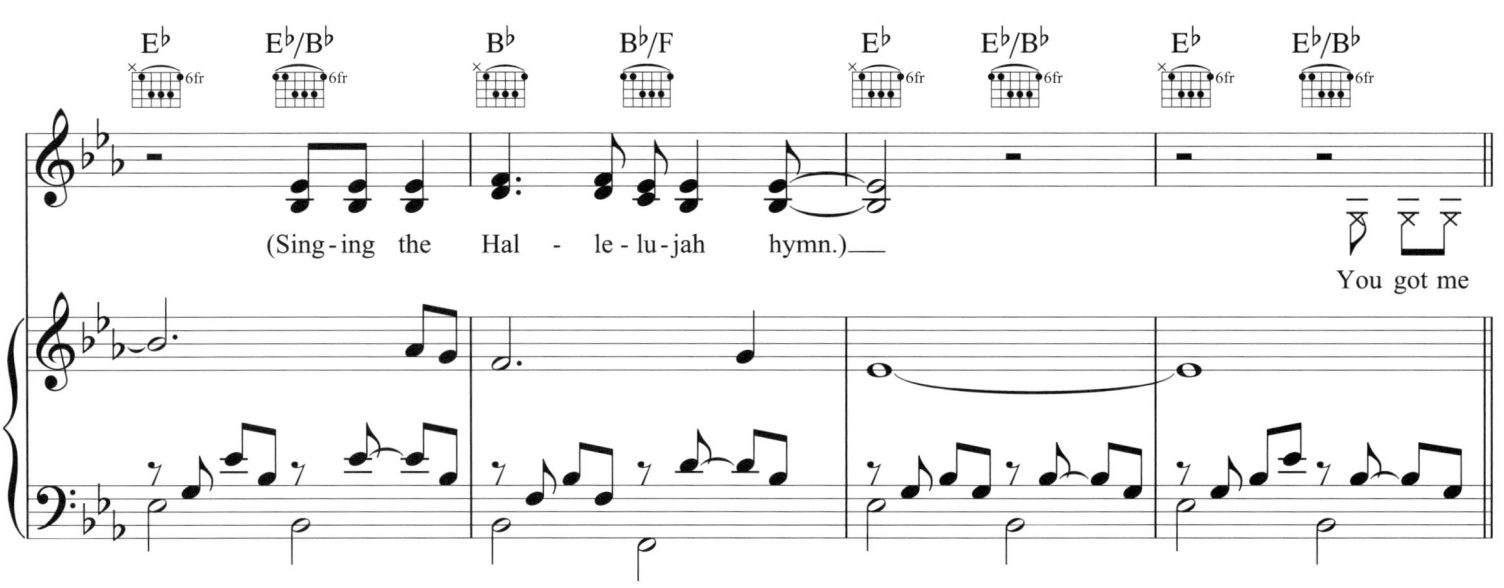

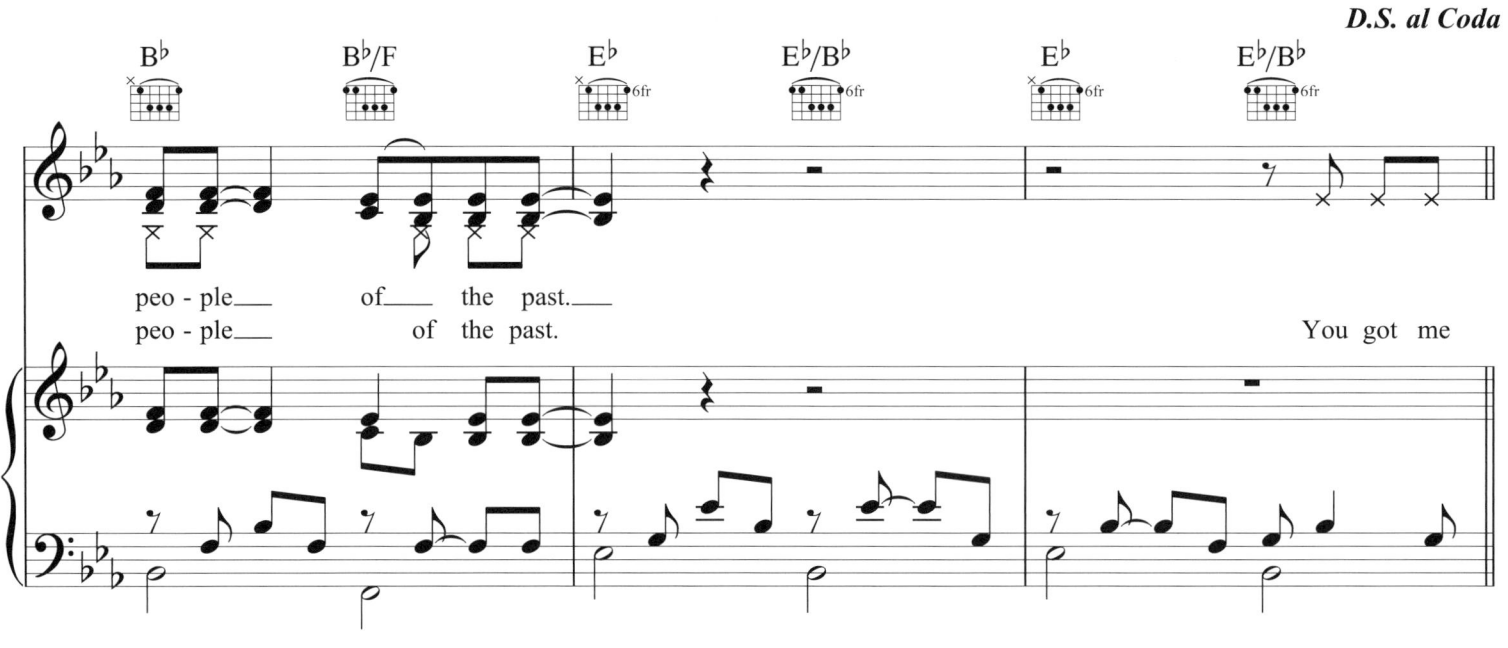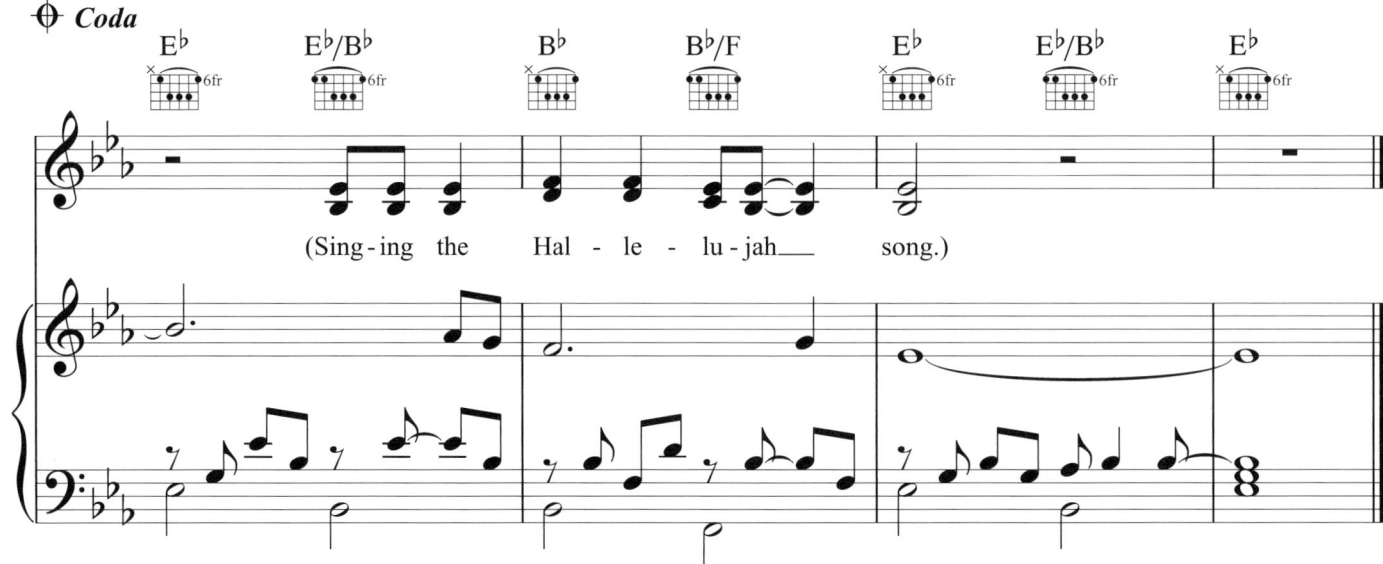

# Bringing you the words and the music

All the latest music in print... rock & pop plus jazz, blues, country, classical and the best in West End show scores.

- Books to match your favourite CDs.

- Book-and-CD titles with high quality backing tracks for you to play along to. Now you can play guitar or piano with your favourite artist... or simply sing along!

- Audition songbooks with CD backing tracks for both male and female singers for all those with stars in their eyes.

- Can't read music? No problem, you can still play all the hits with our wide range of chord songbooks.

- Check out our range of instrumental tutorial titles, taking you from novice to expert in no time at all!

- Musical show scores include *The Phantom Of The Opera*, *Les Misérables*, *Mamma Mia* and many more hit productions.

- DVD master classes featuring the techniques of top artists.

Visit your local music shop or, in case of difficulty, contact the Marketing Department, Music Sales Limited, Newmarket Road, Bury St Edmunds, Suffolk, IP33 3YB, UK
marketing@musicsales.co.uk